A play by
Gary Soto

A Member of Penguin Putnam Inc.

Professional and amateurs are hereby warned
that this play is subject to a royalty.
For information regarding performance rights,
contact BookStop Literary Agency,
67 Meadow View Road, Orinda, California 94563,
(925)254-2668.

Mil gracias to David Chavez, and
un aplauso to the Drama Club of Sanger High School,
pictured on the cover

A PaperStar Book, published in 1999 by Penguin Putnam Books
for Young Readers, 345 Hudson Street, New York, NY 10014.
PaperStar is a registered trademark of The Putnam Berkley Group,Inc.
The PaperStar logo is a trademark of The Putnam Berkley Group, Inc.
Published simultaneously in Canada. Printed in the United States of America.

Library of Congress Cataloging-in-Publication Data
Soto, Gary.   Nerdlandia : a play / Gary Soto.   p.   cm.
Summary: A humorous play in which Martin, a Chicano nerd, undergoes
a transformation with the help of his friends and experiences true love.
Includes a glossary of Spanish words and phrases used in the dialogue.
1. Mexican American youth—Juvenile drama. 2. Young adult drama, American.
[1. Mexican Americans—Drama. 2. Plays.]   I. Title.
PS3569.O72N47   1999   812´.54—dc21   98-37093   CIP   AC
ISBN 0-698-11784-0
30 29 28 27 26 25 24 23 22 21

For the members of Los Lobos—

Steve Berlin
David Hidalgo
Conrad Lozano
Louie Pérez
Cesar Rojas

keep howling

Performance Notes

1. Until Scene 4, Martin should mispronounce the Spanish words and phrases. After his heart transplant, his Spanish should be spoken with a correct accent. At that point, the director has the choice of accenting his name, from Martin to Martín. Change in name pronunciation is optional.

2. The play takes place in Fresno, California, but references to towns, schools, restaurants, famous people, etc., may be changed for local appeal.

3. All music should be uncopyrighted, original, or within the public domain.

A glossary of Spanish words and alang begins on page 86.

Characters

Martin, nerdish boy

Joaquin, *vato loco*

Freddie and **Tito**, humorous *vatos locos*

Ceci, love-struck *chola*

Lupe and **Susana**, *cholas*

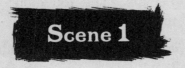

Scene 1

In front of a high school.

(Eyes downcast, Martin, a Chicano nerd, paces. He sports a calculator on his belt, eyeglasses, white shirt with a thin tie, pants hiked up around his chest. He stops when he sees Joaquin, a cholo wannabe who is "tagging" a wall. Joaquin notices Martin.)

Joaquin: Hey, Martin. How come you're making *la jeta*?

(Not wanting to talk, Martin turns away. Joaquin follows him.)

Joaquin: Come on. What's wrong, homes?

Martin: Nothing's wrong. I'm happy.

Joaquin: You ain't happy. What's up with you? *Qué pasó?*

Martin: Really, I'm fine.

(Joaquin sizes up Martin's sadness.)

1

Joaquin: Let me guess. You didn't make the football team? Is that it?

Martin: *(in a squeaky voice)* No, I didn't go out for football.

Joaquin: It's a joke, *ese*. I know you didn't go out for the team. If you had, *pues*, we wouldn't be 0-7. More like 0-100. *(pause)* I got it! You broke your microscope?

(Martin wags his head no.)

Joaquin: Your ant farm got sprayed with Black Flag?

Martin: No, my ant farm is just fine. And so is my goldfish and my hamster.

(Joaquin ponders Martin's reluctance to talk.)

Joaquin: Ever since you and me first met in kindergarten—and I was there two years getting my colors down real good—you been into this science stuff. I used to think that you were all *tapado*, stuck up. But no, I admit it, I was wrong. You're just a nerd. I figure your kind of people—nerds—and my kind of people—*vatos*—got to come together. *(pause)* I know what's wrong.

Your calculator's broke!

Martin: No, my calculator works just fine. But thank you for asking. *(pause)* If I tell you, you won't laugh?

(Joaquin puts on a straight face.)

Joaquin: Laugh? Laugh at the *vato* who helps me in biology? Who whispers in my ear the answers to algebra? Who fills me with history during finals? So what's going down?

Martin: It's my heart.

Joaquin: *Tu corazón?*

Martin: *(mispronouncing Spanish)* Yes, my *corazón*. Love palpitations.

Joaquin: Love palpitations. That's a hard one to fix. *Tú sabes*, when you fool with your heart, it's delicate. You get inside a person and change things around. But sometimes it's got to be done.

Martin: You know how to repair a broken heart?

Joaquin: *Simón!* I'm the surgeon of all heart surgeons, a specialist when it comes to romance. Shoot, last week I was on the cellular phone with Leonardo DiCaprio [or current heart-throb]. The *vato* was all heartbroken. He was crying because his girl dumped him! Right in front of El Pollo Loco.

Martin: DiCaprio? He was crying?

Joaquin: Like a rain cloud.

(Enter two vatos locos—*Freddie and Tito.)*

Joaquin: Mira, here come *nuestros carnales*— Freddie *y* Tito.

(They yuk it up; they shake hands in an unusually complicated, thus comical, raza *style.)*

Freddie: Man, I got carpal tunnel syndrome from these hand shakes. *(to Joaquin)* So what's going down, Joaquin?

Joaquin: Unemployment, crime, *placas*, and Martin's broken heart.

Freddie: Junior Einstein is heartbroken?

Tito: When I saw his long face, I thought his calculator was broke.

Joaquin: That's what I thought, homes.

(They slap palms; they wince in pain from their carpal tunnel syndrome.)

Tito: *(to Joaquin)* Hey, guess what?

Joaquin: *(mocking Tito)* Hey, I don't know.

Tito: Freddie found a part-time job.

Freddie: *(smiling)* Washing dishes in a Chinese restaurant. I'm going to carry on the family tradition.

(Freddie rubs his palms together, as if washing dishes.)

Joaquin: It seems like our *raza* was born to wash dishes. When did you start?

Freddie: I started when I was seven and my mom made me do the forks and spoons.

Joaquin: No, *tonto*, when did you start the job?

Freddie: Oh. I don't start until this other *vato* gets fired. I'm next in line.

Joaquin: But don't take the job right away because I think we got to help Marty.

(Martin walks slowly away.)

Martin: You guys don't have to. I'll recover.

Joaquin: Martin, you always helped us with school, and we—Freddie, Tito, and me—*pues*, we're going to see you through this dark time.

Freddie: That's right! We can't let our homie down.

Tito: You're the future leader of our people . . . plus we need the answers for next week's history quiz. *(pause)* Come on, Marty, smile. Don't be so tight. Show a little teeth.

(The three of them smile big to the audience. Martin starts slowly and then follows suit with a large smile.)

Tito: So who's this girl? Maybe I can talk to her and . . . ask her out myself!

Freddie: *Mira este chavalo. Sinvergüenza!* Right away he wants to step in all *suave. (pause)* Yeah, where does this girl live?

Joaquin: Allright, you jugheads, don't play with Marty. Can't you see he's all *triste y todo?*

Freddie: *Triste.*

Tito: *Triste y todo.*

Martin: Just because I'm a nerd, you're making fun of me. But I have feelings too. I like girls just like you three . . . *vatos*.

Joaquin: Of course you do. Nerds got feelings like the rest of us. In fact, you're the most *suavecito* with a 4.0 at school.

Martin: You're just saying that.

Freddie: It's the truth. Your name is always coming up like pimples.

Martin: They just want me to help them with their homework.

Freddie: Nah, homes! They admire you and your intelligence. In fact, I was kicking down the hallway looking for a free sandwich when I heard Belinda Sanchez say in a low, kitty cat voice, "Martin, what a smooth calculator."

Joaquin: *Híjole*, Belinda can turn on the charm.

Tito: *De veras*! She was panting over that big digital machine on your belt.

Martin: I really appreciate that, *mi carnal*. But I know I'm not a *suavecito*. I'm just another Chicano nerd in America. *(pause)* Can I confide in you three?

(The three vatos look at each other.)

Freddie: Confide? Is that anything like *con safos*?

Tito: Sounds like a cussword. Are you calling us a bad word in nerd language? Because we don't take that, *ese*.

Martin: It means, can I tell you something . . . personal?

(All of them ad-lib, "Yeah, go ahead; let it spill, órale," etc.)

Martin: I was listening to this song yesterday while I was filling my petri dish with bacteria, and *(becoming shy)* . . .

Joaquin: *Y qué?*

Martin: I had a strange sensation that the song was exclusively meant for me.

Joaquin: Songs do that, *qué no?* They bring up all these dark emotions. You get your ride, bump along Blackstone Avenue [or local street], the radio up, the girls eyeing you behind big old layers of mascara. *Híjole*, it's the best experience. What song was you listening to, little Marty?

Martin: I appreciate your asking, *carnal*. I don't recall the title, but it went something like this . . .

(Martin sings in a Frank Sinatra-like croon.)

Martin: *(continuing)* Molecules, fluctuating molecules,/floating in the calculus of our feelings./Molecules, fluctuating molecules/drifting in the strata molecular bonding,/I light you like a Bunsen burner,/study you under the microscope of life,/dissect you like a frog,/my barium chromate, my future wife.

(The three stand shocked by Martin's science-laden song.)

Joaquin: I don't know what that was about, *pero* if it moves you, that's good. Come on, jugheads. Give it up! *Aplauso!* *(pause)* So who's this girl anyhow?

Martin: I can't part with her name. My lips are sealed until the rivers run dry and stars go out like lightbulbs.

Freddie: Stop with the poetry, Junior Einstein.

(Martin mutters her name under his breath. The three of them shout that they can't hear him.)

Martin: *(loudly)* Ceci Cortez!

(Joaquin, Freddie, and Tito, shocked and looking in the direction of the audience, yell out, "Ceci Cortez!")

Joaquin: Ceci, that wild heartbreaker? The best-looking girl in our corner of the planet.

Freddie: *Fíjate*, Marty. We got experience with ordinary girls, but good-looking ones, *pues*, we don't know a lot.

Joaquin: Freddie's right. We're all stupid when it comes to items like Ceci.

Freddie: Plus her old man, Sleepy. He would tear us up if he found us trying to set you up with Ceci.

Tito: That's right. We ain't going to mess with Sleepy's girl.

Joaquin: Sleepy ain't nowhere. I'll get my homies to do some of this.

(Freddie and Tito throw a few boxing jabs.)

Joaquin: And some of this.

(Freddie and Tito karate-kick.)

Joaquin: And some of these bad karate chops.

(Freddie and Tito chop the air.)

Joaquin: I would lay him out like a Tortilla—flat.

(Offstage, Sleepy's voice rumbles, "No one better mess with my girl." The three vatos—Joaquin, Freddie, and Tito—huddle together in fear.)

Freddie: Joaquin, you better rethink the game plan. *(pause)* I remember when Sleepy grabbed me by the throat.

Tito: I remember. You had just got a drink of water at the playground. He took you by your throat like a burrito and the *agua* squirted all out.

(Tito pantomimes water leaping from his mouth.)

Joaquin: You're probably right. Sleepy's pretty scary.

Martin: You mean you won't help?

(The boys, sizing up Martin's pathetic situation, moan, "Of course we'll try, homes; sure, why not; órale, we'll stand by you," etc.)

11

Joaquin: You really got the microscope on her, Junior Einstein?

Martin: I think about her all the time. Yesterday when I was plotting the equation to the hyperbola of X minus two times the quantity of the radius of pi, I just floated off into space.

Joaquin: That's pretty heavy. But instead of Ceci, maybe Julieta or Laura or Ana or maybe the new girl from El Salvador. The one that pushes the little *paleta* cart on Saturdays.

Martin: No, my *corazón* is set on Ceci. I dream about her and I even . . .

Joaquin: Even what?

Martin: Hug my pillow.

Joaquin: *Chihuahua*! You got it serious, homeboy. Are you kissing the pillow *también*?

(Martin nods his head yes.)

Freddie: *(pointing offstage)* Hey, look who's coming!

Joaquin: Let's hide.

(Martin, Freddie, and Joaquin hide. Ceci, Susana, and Lupe enter stage. The three girls walk across the stage

with attitude; Lupe sniffs the air.)

Lupe: You smell something?

Ceci: *(sniffing the air)* Boys. *(sniffing the air a second time)* Three, no, four boys.

Susana: *(excited)* Oooooh. And I thought we were just going over to the library to study.

Ceci: We are. So forget them. Dudes are nothing but trouble.

(The girls leave, and the boys once again show themselves.)

Martin: How come we had to hide?

Joaquin: Practice. We got to practice hiding from girls. Like ninjas. In the future, they'll be all over us.

Freddie: Girls will be all over us?

(Joaquin pats Freddie's shoulder.)

Joaquin: Well, some of us, Freddie. Not all of us.

(Tito looks offstage where the girls had walked off.)

13

Tito: Yeah, I known Ceci since she was real little. In fact . . . *(stops)*

Freddie: *Qué?* Spill it!

Tito: I can't tell you guys.

Joaquin: *Chale.* We're your homies!

Freddie: *(imitating) Chale.* We're your homies!

(Joaquin gives him a look of "be quiet!")

Joaquin: Your problem is our problem. Unless it means that we might get beat up. Then you're on your own.

Tito: *(babyish)* She stole my bike with trainer wheels, beat me up and . . .

Joaquin: Let it out. It's not good to keep these repressed emotions.

Tito: *(sniveling)* And Ceci called me a bad word.

(Joaquin and Freddie let out a small laugh.)

Tito: It's not funny.

Joaquin: That's right. It's not funny. A girl who steals your trainer-wheel bike will scar you for life.

Freddie: What did Ceci call you?

Tito: I can't tell you.

Joaquin: What do you mean you can't tell us? We've known each other since we were in Pampers—little *vatos locos* kicking up trouble in our strollers.

(The three of them wait for Tito to speak.)

Tito: *(with pretend tears)* She called me the 'c' word.

Joaquin: The 'c' word?

Tito: She called me a . . . *caca*.

Freddie: That's cold!

Joaquin: *Ay*, Tito, don't take it hard. Chin up. Be a Marine. What you suffered is in the past. Look at Marty here. He's hurting big-time right now.

Martin: It's true, Tito. I'm hurting here right in my *corazón*.

Tito: Thanks, Junior Einstein. You and me understand how cruel Ceci can be.

(Offstage, Sleepy's voice rumbles, "You better leave my girl alone.")

15

Martin: *(to offstage voice)* But Sleepy, I love her. Let me show you how. *(singing)* "Molecules, fluctuating molecules—"

(Freddie cuts him off.)

Freddie: No, Marty. You'll just make Sleepy mad singing a song to his girl.

(The four pace, thinking of their precarious situation.)

Joaquin: *Pues*, we're going to rebuild your body. Drop a new heart in you.

Tito: Like a new engine block?

Joaquin: That's right. Like a new engine.

Freddie: We'll get a bucket of Bondo and fill you in, especially that hollow chest of yours.

Tito: Bondo's cool, huh?

Freddie: Yeah. It reminds me of my years at the playground when I used to work with Play-Doh. Squeezing the stuff between your *dedos* like *masa*, making little ashtrays, little Virgin Lupes, statues of Power Rangers, these bad-looking lowriders.

Tito: Remember we used to make plaster-of-paris masks?

Freddie: And yours was so ugly it made babies cry.

Tito: *(proudly)* Yeah, my mask was ugly, huh?

Freddie: *Muy* ugly. Ah, the good old days at the playground.

Joaquin: Listen, the way I figure, instead of the heart transplant, we go simple.

Tito: Simple! We're good at being simple.

(Freddie and Tito slap palms.)

Joaquin: We'll set Marty up with some tough-looking *garras*.

Freddie: Khakis and a Pendleton.

Tito: Like work on the outer self first, huh?

Joaquin: That's it, homes, the outer self. Then if that don't work, we'll work on the inner self. *(pause)* You know, we should trip down to La Raza Mall.

Tito: I heard of the place. They got that restaurant called Tacos-R-Us.

Joaquin: And *una tienda que se llama* Big y Huango.

Freddie: Plus the pawn shop You Snooze You Lose.

Joaquin: *(to Martin)* You ready to check this place out?

Martin: I'll do anything to become a *suavecito*.

Joaquin: OK, then, *vámonos*. Let's get out of here.

(The four leave. Lights dim, then darken.)

Scene 2

In front of the high school.

(Lights come up immediately. Enter Ceci, Lupe, and Susana.)

Susana: Girl, what's wrong with you? I mean, he wears a calculator on his belt!

Lupe: And his *pantalones* are all the way up to his throat. Like they're choking him or something.

Susana: And did you hear what he wants to start? *(Ceci shakes her head)* A club for people into ant farms.

Lupe: *Qué loco!* He's a funny dude.

Ceci: But he's sweet.

Lupe: So! If you want something sweet, buy a soda.

Ceci: I'm not talking thirst, girl. I'm talking about a guy I can trust. He's better than that no-good Sleepy. He said he was going to the library.

Lupe: *(eyeing Susana)* Instead he was with you know who.

Ceci: *(angrily at Susana)* Yeah—her! Susana!

Susana: I'm sorry. He said that you and him broke up. I didn't know. Honest, Ceci. I'm not the kind of *chola* who goes out with her best friend's dude.

Lupe: *La flaca's* telling the truth. She was really sorry, Ceci. She cried exactly ninety-six *lágrimas*. Huh, Susana?

Susana: It's true. I spilled them tears all over my bedroom. And I felt so bad that I let Lupe pull my hair for an hour.

Lupe: *De veras.* I punished that girl.

Ceci: *(tenderly)* I know. I don't mean to be hard. But it still hurts. *(pause)* I was a fool to trust that *ratón* Sleepy. And now look at him. In juvie for putting his name in wet cement. How stupid!

(Offstage, Sleepy's voice rumbles, "You better not go out with Junior Einstein.")

Ceci: *(to offstage voice)* You can't tell me what to

do. We're through, Sleepy. You're locked away and out of my life.

(The girls pace.)

Lupe: It's like the bad experience I had last year.

Ceci: Sleepy hit on you too?

(Lupe grows silent. She walks away from her friends.)

Ceci: What? What happened?

Lupe: Remember when I was in love with Little Ray? And I begged him to let me wear his Raiders jacket?

Ceci: *(frustrated)* Do you have to bring this up again?

Lupe: And I lost it, his jacket. The one his mother had bought him when she won a hundred *bolas* from the lottery. He made me feel so low!

Susana: *Cállate* already.

Lupe: *(with tears)* Then I found it under the bleachers. The jacket his mom bought!

Susana: Get over it, girl.

Lupe: It was all dirty and messed up.

Ceci: Put it behind you! That was last year, not yesterday.

Lupe: *(sniffling)* Alright. I won't talk about it anymore. It's gone. It belongs to the past. We must look toward the future. *(pause)* Then he made me pay for the cleaning bill and told all his friends about it.

Susana: *Ay, Dios.* Every time we talk about romance, you bring up Little Ray and his stupid Raiders jacket.

Ceci: *Vatos* are cruel.

Susana: *Malos* two-timers.

Lupe: Low-down *ratones*.

Susana: *Huevones* to the ninth degree!

(The girls start, one by one, to look out into the audience, noticing the boys.)

Ceci: *Espérate.* Wait a second. Let's not be hasty. *(pointing at a boy)* That one *allá*. He's *fino*.

Susana: *(pointing at another boy)* He's fine too. That *ratoncito* in the front row.

Ceci: *Y el güero* over there. I like your eyes, my little *empanada*.

Lupe: Wait a second. We're getting sidetracked. Guys will do that, make us forget about what's really important.

(Offstage, Sleepy's voice rumbles, "You better not go out with Junior Einstein.")

Ceci: *(to offstage voice) Cállate!* I'll do what I want. You don't own me or nothing. *(to girls)* He thinks I should do what he wants. Forget him!

Susana: Maybe you're right, Ceci. What you need is a guy who is faithful.

Lupe: Kind!

Susana: Intelligent!

Ceci: I like that. A guy who is kind, faithful, and smart. And looks shouldn't matter that much. Even if he's got braces on his teeth.

Susana: I remember this girl telling me that she was making out with this guy with braces.

Lupe: So?

Susana: Braces with these rubber bands. And

when he and the girl were making out, one of his rubber bands shot in her mouth.

Lupe: *Asco!*

(The girls pace.)

Ceci: Looks help, I agree. But for me, personally, I want a guy I can trust.

(Offstage, Sleepy's voice rumbles, "You can trust me, *chola*.")

Ceci: *(to offstage voice)* Shut up, I said!

Lupe: Dudes, they're always promising things.

Susana: That's right. They promise to write love letters, but do they write them? *Mentirosos!* I remember this guy from Kerman [or local town]. We danced and danced and got pretty close in the parking lot. Julio was, *chihuahua*, one hot *tamal*.

Lupe: I think I went out with that guy. He's got a ponytail, no?

Susana: *(eagerly)* And a cute little scar on his chin?

Lupe: And these cowboy boots?

(The two of them click their heels together.)

Susana: He's a real good kisser, huh?

Lupe: Yeah, but he kissed me first!

Susana: He was only breaking his lips in for me, girl. It was just something for him to do while he waited for me to come around!

(Lupe glares at Susana, then turns away.)

Lupe: Guys are so cruel.

Susana: Deceitful.

(The girls pace, fretting over their boy problems.)

Lupe: We got to be careful about guys.

Susana: What do you mean?

(Lupe throws a frightened look around the stage.)

Lupe: Did you ever hear about that scary date, about how some girl who met this guy who was really a . . . I better not say.

Susana: What?

Lupe: *Pues*, he was really a chicken.

Ceci: What are you talking about, *loca*?

Lupe: *Tú sabes,* that *muchacha* who fell in love with this guy at the dance. A club called El Rancho.

Susana: And the lights went out. And when they came back on—

Lupe: *(butting in)* Let me tell it! It's my story. *(to the audience)* She was this country girl from the state of Monterrey. She was shy and pretty like me. Her parents were all strict and stuff, and wouldn't let her go nowhere. But then she sneaked out of the house to go clubbing.

(Ceci and Susana feign dancing.)

Lupe: *(continuing)* She was having a good time. She was dancing with this good-looking dude with a long neck.

(Ceci and Susana stick their necks in and out like chickens.)

Lupe: *(continuing)* And the lights went out.

(Ceci and Susana scream.)

Lupe: *(continuing)* And one of her earrings fell off.

(The girls gaze down at the floor in search of the earring.)

Lupe: She bent to pick it up. Right then, she saw that her *novio* had a pair of chicken legs.

(Ceci and Susana scream, "Piernas de pollo!")

Lupe: *En serio.* Her date was a chicken.

(Ceci and Susana chuckle.)

Ceci: I'm not worried about Martin. I already know he's a chicken. Heck, I could beat him up easy if I wanted.

(Offstage, Sleepy's voice rumbles, "You better not go out with him, Ceci.")

Ceci: That does it! *No más!*

(Ceci stomps offstage. We hear the sound of punches, kicks, slaps, moans, etc. Susana and Lupe cringe from the noise. Silence. Ceci returns, breathing hard and rubbing her knuckles.)

Susana: Is everything OK? He's not hurt, is he?

(Ceci cuts mad stares at the audience.)

Ceci: We just had a little talk. We decided to end our relationship.

Susana: What's that in your hand?

(Susana takes a few strands of hair from Ceci's hand. She lets the strands flutter to the ground.)

Lupe: Looks like Sleepy's hair. *Híjole*, you're one nasty cat. *(pause)* You really like the little nerd?

Ceci: *(snapping)* His name is Martin, not nerd! We shouldn't put him down because he's smart!

Lupe: OK. I'm sorry.

Susana: If you like him, it's OK with me. Huh, Lupe?

Lupe: Sure.

(The girls glance at the mailbox scrawled with placas.*)*

Lupe: *Mira!* Look at these love *placas*!

Ceci: *Placas* for days. Some of them are really old—1957, 62, 66, 73 . . .

(They examine the mailbox.)

Lupe: Check this out, homegirls. Joaquin *con* Susana.

Ceci: Is that the Joaquin from school?

Lupe: That's him allright. He spelled "eternally" all wrong. I–n–t–e–r–n–a–l–l–y.

(The three study the names on the mailbox.)

Ceci: *(to Susana)* Joaquin is pretty cute. You got eyes for him, *o qué?*

Susana: Maybe. Maybe not. But . . . probably maybe.

Lupe: *Cuidado!* Joaquin hangs out with those tontos, Freddie and Tito.

Ceci: Freddie and Tito? Didn't some tough homeboys lock them in a locker for the weekend?

Lupe: That's them. A couple of soft tacos!

Susana: But Joaquin is cute, even if he can't spell. *(to Ceci) Pues,* how are you going to get your guy?

Lupe: Yeah, how are you going to snag Junior Einstein?

Ceci: I'm going to the mall. I'm going to change my image. *(dreamily)* There's that store called Nerdstrom's. They sell nerd dresses and nerd shoes and glasses thick as magnifying glasses. Plus lots of science stuff.

Susana: No, girl! You can't shop there!

Lupe: Those are hecka ugly clothes.

Susana: *(pleading)* You're one of us!

Ceci: I'm sorry to let you *cholas* down. But I'm going to get my nerd. I mean, didn't you ever want to be, like, someone else?

Susana: No.

Ceci: Think about it.

Susana: I wanted to be like . . . never mind.

Ceci: Come on, tell us.

Susana: Well, I wanted to be like . . . Barbie.

Ceci: There you go. That's nice.

Susana: But a brown Barbie. A shade lighter than chicken *mole*.

Lupe: I got a confession *también*.

Ceci: You wanted to be like Barbie too?

Lupe: You know how we dream. Pretend? I wanted to be like Selena.

Ceci: That's real nice. Her *música es la mejor.*

Susana: Maybe you're right. It's OK to be someone else, to try something different.

Ceci: *Es la verdad.* And for me, *pues*, Nerdstrom's is the place. I'm going to hook my man.

Lupe: Like fishing, huh?

Ceci: That's right. Like a fish, *un gran pescado.*

(Ceci casts an invisible fishing pole and Lupe and Susana pretend to bite. Ceci hauls them offstage. Lights dim, then darken.)

La Raza Mall.

(Joaquin leads Tito into the mall, a failed venture. There are "cerrado" signs on the House of Curls, Victor's Auto Supplies, Sal's Barber Shop #2, and Big y Huango. La Panadería de Jalisco, Cheese and Shoes, Discount Toylandia, We Cash Sus Cheques, Tacos-R-Us, The Suave Shop, and Nerdstrom's and look run down. The Suave Shop and Nerdstrom's are next to each other. A stuffed parrot sitting in the window of the pet store called Pet-a-Pet. Litter sprinkles the street.)

Joaquin: Times are hard.

Tito: Looks like my backyard, all *rasqüachi*.

(They walk around the stage sizing up the mall.)

Tito: *(pointing at auto supplies)* That's where I got my dad his jumper cables for Christmas.

Joaquin: *(pointing)* That's where I got my first haircut.

(Tito goes to the bakery and sucks in the smells.)

Tito: *Mi abuelita* worked at this *panadería*.

Joaquin: Did she used to bring home pig cookies?

Tito: *Claro que sí!* I'd bite off their toes and legs and then their heads. It was like a horror movie, my teeth going like chain saws.

(Martin enters.)

Joaquin: We been waiting. Where you been?

Martin: I went to go see Sleepy.

Joaquin: Sleepy?

Martin: I told him that I love Ceci with all *mi corazón*.

Tito: And you're still alive? You ain't hurt or nothing?

Martin: I'm OK. But you should have seen Sleepy. Someone had pummeled him. He had some serious abrasions and contusions.

Joaquin: Like he got in a fight?

(Joaquin nods his head.)

Tito: Juvie's a hard reality.

Martin: I told him that I love Ceci more than my goldfish Melvin, and he just smiled. It was surprising. He said, "Thanks, man. You take her."

Joaquin: That's weird. Letting her go like that.

Martin: That's what he said just before his nose started bleeding and he went unconscious.

Joaquin: Must have been some fight. *(pause)* Where's Freddie?

Martin: He called me and said that he going to join the three of us right after he gets off work.

Tito: The *vato* got the job already?

Martin: *Sí, en el restaurante chino.*

(Freddie enters, wearing an apron and swinging a box of Chinese takeout.)

Freddie: First day in the shop, and they let me off early. *(wagging the box at his friends) Fíjate*, I got cookies for you dudes.

(The three of them take the cookies and one by one they crack them open and read their fortunes.)

Freddie: Mine says, "You are good-looking, a leader, *y muy macho.*" *(smiling) Es la verdad!* This cookie wouldn't lie to a homie like me.

Tito: Mine says that I will change the world.

Freddie: How you going to change the world if you can't even change your *chones*?

(Freddie and Tito slap palms and laugh.)

Joaquin: Jugheads! That's enough Chicano humor. *(to Martin) Y tú,* Junior Einstein? What's the word?

(Martin appears downcast.)

Martin: It says . . . one day I will become Mr. Universe.

(The parrot in the shop window signs, "Chale.")

Tito: These fortune cookies *son mentirosas.*

Freddie: You can say that again.

(The parrot sings, "Chale, chale, chale!" Baffled, the boys look around, wondering who's speaking.)

Joaquin: Was that you, Freddie?

Freddie: *Nel.* I thought it was you.

Joaquin: *(looking about)* It wasn't me. The place is throwing out some bad vibes *y sustos.* All these businesses that closed up and laid *un gran pedo.*

(The parrot sings, "puro pedo!")

Tito: Who said that?

Freddie: You calling us bad names, *ese? Pues,* come out, *vato.* Show us *su cara!* We'll throw some *chingasos!* Tito, you take him.

Tito: I don't want to fight. The last time I got into some nasty *pleitos* I got all messed up. That'll teach me to mouth off to *mi abuelita.* That *vieja's* tough.

(Wind or eerie noise blows, then stops.)

Joaquin: *(spooked) Es el espíritu de un* mall in foreclosure.

(Wind noise blows again.)

Joaquin: *(continuing)* It's kind of spooky here, *qué no? (pause)* Hey, did I ever tell you about this vato from Mexico who could change himself into a wolf? *Un lobo.*

Tito: I heard of *el vato.* He used to do this transmission thing, no?

Joaquin: Transformation, not transmission, *tonto. (pause)* Anyhow, this dude used to hit all the clubs, and when he saw some *chica* he was hot for, he changed himself into a wolf.

Freddie: No, it wasn't a wolf. The dude was a chicken with chicken legs. *Tú sabes?*

(Joaquin pounds his fist against his forehead.)

Joaquin: That's right. He had these really skinny legs, like Junior Einstein, and when the lights went out during a slow dance . . .

(Freddie and Tito pretend to slow dance, then snap back into their regular postures.)

Joaquin: *(continuing)* he turned into a real chicken, no? I remember that *cuento* from when I was a kid.

Tito: My mom used to scare me with that story. Then she would serve chicken enchiladas and tell us that it was the chicken man we were grubbing on.

Freddie: Your mom's always been a joker!

(The parrot sings, "Chale, ese!") ·

Joaquin: It's that voice again. This place is haunted.

(Martin notices the parrot and picks him up.)

Martin: It's the bird. He can speak.

Freddie: Yeah, he speaks gooder than me.

(The parrot says, "Chale!" "Órale pues," "Puro pedo!" etc. The three vatos look at the parrot, then Martin.)

Martin: He's a bearded macaw from, I believe, the upper Amazon.

Joaquin: He crossed a couple of borders? He's illegal? If no one owns him, let's snag the dude. I mean, the store is all closed up.

Freddie: *El pobrecito* is probably all hungry. Who's got sunflower seeds?

(Tito pulls out a bag of sunflower seeds and places it under the parrot's beak.)

Martin: Look at him eat.

Joaquin: He's a real Chicano bird. Look at him eat up these sunflower seeds. He's grubbing the shells *y todo*. (pause as they watch the bird) Hey, any of you dudes eat a bird before?

(The parrot squawks.)

Martin: Joaquin! Be sensitive! He's our new friend. We shouldn't talk about eating birds in front of him.

Joaquin: I'm sorry, Tweety Bird. OK, no stories about birds fried into *taquitos*.

(Tito turns over the bags of sunflower seeds, indicating that the parrot has eaten them all.)

Freddie: *(pointing to a band on his leg.) Mira!* The dude's got a little bracelet on his *pata*.

Joaquin: What does it say?

Freddie: *(looking closely)* It says, "Go, Chargers!" [or local team]

Joaquin: This is one cool bird! He's into sports! *(to bird)* Give me a low claw!

(Joaquin and the parrot rake claws.)

Martin: Can we see about my new clothes? That's why we're here, isn't it?

Joaquin: Marty is right. Let's hurry up and get him dressed up in his new *trajes*.

(The parrot sings, "Órale, carnales. Vámonos! Vivan los Chargers!" They enter The Suave Shop. Sound of wind for thirty seconds; then it fades. Enter Ceci, Susana, and Lupe, all of them looking about, amazed at the condition of La Raza Mall.)

Ceci: What happened to this place? Everything is closed.

(The girls size up the mall.)

Ceci: I remember that *panadería*. After church, my mom used to buy me *pan dulce* and chocolate milk. It was nice back then, but now it's all

. . .feo y rasqüachi.

Susana: Even *los* winos moved out.

(The girls look around the mall.)

Susana: *(pointing at sign)* And wasn't that a crazy business—Cheese and Shoes!

Lupe: *Queso y zapatos*! I remember when you bought two pairs of shoes—

Susana: *(butting in)* And he would say, "I'm going to cut the cheese, *muchacha*!" And laugh. He was *muy loco, el viejo*.

Ceci: I remember buying these little white shoes for my first communion. I felt so pretty that all I did was look at my shoes as I walked down the aisle.

Susana: You used to be all religious back then?

Ceci: Not really. My mom used to send me to church alone. But it was boring! So instead of going to church I went to Safeway for a soda and a candy bar.

Susana: *Era muy mala, esa.*

Ceci: I know, brown girl. I was bad. I spent the

money Mom gave for the poor. I would look at magazines, gobble up my goodies, and when I thought an hour had gone by, *pues*, I went home like this.

(Ceci presses her hands together in prayer.)

Lupe: Your mom never found out?

Ceci: No. When she asked what church was about I'd just say . . . heaven and stuff. *(pause)* This place is gone. What it needs is a new Latina vision. In fact, I was thinking that we three should start a business.

Susana: Like what?

Lupe: *(excited)* I got it! We could do nails. Just think of all the *cholas* in *el barrio* who need sharpening.

(Lupe rakes the air with her fingernails.)

Ceci: Forget nails and hair and babysitting and stuff like that. We should get into engineering. Or become doctors. We could help the *mocoso* babies when they come in all sick.

Lupe: We ain't cut out for that, girl.

Ceci: *Por qué no*? Just because we're *cholas* doesn't mean we can't do something profound.

Susana: I never heard you use the word "profound" before.

Ceci: I'm using it now. And I'm serious. We should do more than sit around sipping sodas and eating sunflower seeds.

Lupe: You mean it, huh?

Ceci: That's why I'm going in there. There's going to be a new me.

(Ceci enters Nerdstrom's. Lupe and Susana look at one another, hesitant to go into the store.)

Lupe: *(to Susana)* Now you.

Susana: *Nel, pastel!* You go next.

Lupe: OK, but you better not chicken out. Ceci needs our help.

(Lupe disappears into the store.)

Susana: *(to the audience)* I don't want any of you spreading *chisme* about me shopping at Nerdstrom's. What will my *chola* friends say?

They'll make fun of me. So don't say anything! OK?

(Susana disappears, closing the door behind her. Seconds later, out step Freddie and Joaquin from The Suave Shop.)

Joaquin: Come on out, Tito!

(Tito steps out of the store with the parrot dressed in dark shades, a tiny Pendleton, a white T-shirt, a bandana, etc.)

Tito: The bird's raw.

(The parrot sings, "Órale!")

Joaquin: And you too, Junior Einstein. Let's check out *sus garras. (to the audience)* He's a little scared of making his *entrada*. It's kind of like a *quinceañera* for the *vatito*.

Freddie: I remember when I got my first Pendleton, and I was kind of shy wearing it around, looking all *suavecito*, like I was all bad. Yeah, bad on my trainer-wheel bike. So I can understand how Marty feels now. *(yelling)* Come out, *ese*. Show the *gente* your pride!

(Martin, dressed in gang garb, comes out with a large radio on his shoulders. He struts around with his pants pulled up.)

Martin: *(to Joaquin in mispronounced Spanish) Quibo, hermano! Qué pasa?*

Joaquin: It's the same ol' Martin. Pull your pants down.

(Martin starts to take them off.)

Joaquin: I mean lower your pants, not take them off. Don't wear them all the way to your throat.

(Martin lowers his pants to a comfortable position.)

Martin: *Escuche la música.*

(Martin switches on classsical music.)

Joaquin: *Chihuahua!* You can take the nerd into *el barrio*, but you can't force *el barrio* into the nerd.

Martin: *(lowering volume of music)* I'm still the same, huh?

Joaquin: You're still the same, Marty. I guess I got to operate. Drop in a certified *corazón de Aztlán*.

Martin: Will it hurt?

Joaquin: The operation? *Nel.* I've done it before, made this—

Tito: *(butting in)* Transmission.

Joaquin: No, transformation, *tonto.* Come on. *Ven.* Let's get to work.

(Joaquin, Freddie, and Tito leave in a suave *shuffle, followed by Martin, who is searching the stations on his radio.)*

(Lupe, then Susana, exit from Nerdstrom's.)

Lupe: She's changed.

Susana: Yeah, did you see how she wiggled into that big old nasty girdle and stepped into that weird dress?

Lupe: It's like going out on Halloween. She's in costume.

(Ceci exits from Nerdstrom's, dressed to the max as a

nerd. But in spite of her new look, she still has an attitude.)

Ceci: *Qué piensas?* Do I look like a nerd?

(Susana and Lupe turn Ceci around several times, taking in her appearance.)

Susana: You look different.

Ceci: But do I, *tú sabes*, seem different? Am I a nerd girl? And don't lie, *flaca*, or, *pues*, I'll get real mad.

Susana: You sound the same, like us. Huh, Lupe?

Lupe: *Es la verdad.* You look different, *pero* you seem like the same old chola. *(pause)* I know. You forgot something in the store.

(Lupe rushes back into the store.)

Ceci: I wonder if nerds dance. I'll give up everything, but not clubbing.

Susana: *(pondering)* I seen some nerds dance before. They go like this . . .

(Susana goes into a hippie-style wild nonsense dance.)

47

Susana: *Y nosotros.* We go like this . . .

(Susana imitates a slow dance.)

Ceci: There is a difference, huh?

(Lupe returns from the store with a microscope.)

Lupe: I think this is what you're missing. What you do is look in this end and check out all the *insectos.* Then you become a nerd, *yo creo.*

(Ceci peers into microscope.)

Susana: What do you see?

Ceci: I see, I see . . . my eyelashes.

Susana: You got to open your eyes real big. Like this.

(Susana bugs out her eyes at the audience. Ceci does the same and then lowers her face to the microscope.)

Lupe: What do you see?

Ceci: Something long. It's really scary. It's . . . my fingernail.

(Flustered, Ceci gives up.)

Susana: You got to work at being a nerd. It just don't happen over night, *tú sabes*? Like us. We weren't born *cholas*. We had to work on it.

Ceci: You're right . . .

Lupe: Don't give up. As they say, you can take *la chola* out of *el barrio, pero* you can't take *el barrio* out of *la chola*. It's going to take a while.

Ceci: *Bien.* I'm going home to practice being a nerd.

(The three leave the stage. Lights dim, then darken.)

Scene 4

In front of the school.

(Lights come up on the three boys as they are huddled around a school bench, their makeshift operating table. A heart sits on the bench wrapped in butcher paper. On another school bench sit a battery and a pair of jumper cables, along with a Pendleton. The boys hover over the table like surgeons. Martin faces the audience.)

Martin: How many of you ever wanted to be someone else? Be a wide receiver, or a forward on the soccer team. *(yelling like a soccer announcer)* Gooooooooooooooooooal! *(pause)* Or wanted to play tennis, except your friends would make fun of you in those white *pantalones*? Ignore them! This is about becoming someone else. It's like Halloween, like when you put on a mask and go door-to-door with your new identity. It's about putting on another face. That's what it's about.

(He turns and lies down on a school bench.)

Martin: *(to Joaquin)* I'm ready.

(Martin crosses himself. Joaquin examines Freddie's hands.)

Joaquin: Did you wash your *manos*?

Freddie: *Simón!*

Joaquin: Like when?

Freddie: Like yesterday.

Joaquin: OK. Just checking.

(Joaquin turns his attention to Martin. The operation begins.)

Joaquin: Grease.

Freddie: Grease!

(Joaquin combs a big glob of pomade into Martin's hair and rubs the remainder on his own hair.)

Joaquin: Tattoo.

Freddie: Tattoo!

(Joaquin stencils a tattoo on Martin's chest or arm.)

51

Joaquin: Bondo for chest and arms.

Freddie: Bondo for chest and arms!

(Joaquin takes a bucket of Bondo and pretends to slap it onto the patient's chest and arms. Tito dabs at Joaquin's sweaty brow.)

Joaquin: *Un gorro.*

Freddie: *Un gorro!*

(Freddie takes the gorro off Tito's head and hands it to Joaquin, who slips it onto Martin's head.)

Joaquin: *Fíjate!* Give me the jar of Chicano magnetism.

Freddie: Jar of Chicano magnetism!

(Freddie works a little into his armpits.)

Joaquin: Tito! *El corazón.*

(Tito unwraps the heart from the butcher paper, sniffs it, and makes a face at it. He pretends to fit the heart into the body.)

Joaquin: *(continuing)* Jumper cables.

Tito: *Sí, jefe!*

(Tito drags the jumper cables to the operating table.)

Freddie: Cables connected. Turn it over.

(The sound of a car turning over. Martin wakes, legs shaking rhythmically. Music booms like thunder. He stands up, all suave. He is wearing his Pendleton with padded shoulders. He struts for ten to fifteen seconds, playing up his machismo.)

Freddie: Check out Junior Einstein!

Tito: The homie is a cool bomb.

Martin: Cut with the Junior Einstein. *(with perfect Spanish accent)* Soy Martin Pablo Alvarez Gonzalez de Vaca.

Freddie: *Por qué el* long name?

Tito: What, you don't know *tu papi*, so you taking a stab at it?

(Freddie and Tito laugh; Martin walks over and collars them with his pinkies.)

Martin: You saying something about *mi familia*?

(Martin shoves them away. Pause as the two boys collect themselves.)

Joaquin: I put too much Bondo in his arms?

Freddie: *(in a squeaky voice)* Maybe so. *(clearing voice)* I guess we can't play no more with Junior Einstein . . . I mean, Martin Pablo Alvarez Gonzalez de Vaca.

Tito: Or laugh about his ant farm.

Freddie: Or his petri dish.

Tito: Or pull his pants down in gym.

(Martin struts around.)

Martin: I like this new image. Grease in my hair, a tattoo, *mi gorro*, some little rolling r's as in *"perrito."*

Tito: What about your Chicano magnetism?

Martin: *(sniffing armpits)* That too, homie. *(pause)* Fíjate.

Freddie: *Sí, jefito!*

Martin: I'm on a journey.

Joaquin: A journey?

Martin: Do I have to repeat myself, *o qué*? I said "journey," *huevón*. Clean your ears.

(The three poke a finger in their ears.)

Freddie: Is it far away, this journey? My mom won't let me go past the 7-Eleven on Tulare Street [or local street].

Martin: This journey doesn't arrive. It's something in your heart, something ethereal. I'm on a journey called love.

Joaquin: *(to Freddie and Tito)* I think we added too much Chicano magnetism. He sounds a little spacey, *el vato*.

Tito: I ain't going to hang around. I'm out of here. *(to Martin)* Hey, I got to go home and do the dishes. Plus this place you're talking about seems *muy lejos*.

Martin: It's not far, vato. It's right here—*aquí!* *(pounding his heart)* Let's walk.

Tito: I can't. My mom's waiting for me to do the dishes.

Freddie: That's right. Tito's going to wash and I'm going to dry.

(They start to tiptoe away.)

Martin: You guys ain't going nowhere. Fall in line. *(the three fall in line)* Now walk, *tontos*.

(Music plays. They strut across the stage, hands in pockets and looking like suavecitos. They stop and hang out. They kneel down, like gang-bangers, as the music fades.)

Joaquin: I don't know about you *vatos*, but my knees are killing me.

(They stand up; Martin still looks cool.)

Martin: Now check me out! I got the walk down, my hair, *mis trajes, y todo*. But you know, I'm not sure what to say. I don't know if I could take it if Ceci turns me down.

Joaquin: That's the easy part. All you got to do when you see Ceci is, well, you know, *este*, like, uh . . . tell him, Freddie!

Freddie: All you got to do is walk up real slow, like a turtle, and, *pues*, you know, *como, entonces* . . . tell him, Tito!

Tito: A piece of cake, bro. Tell her that she's got

pretty eyes and let's get down and get married.

Joaquin: That's the head-on-collision approach. *(pause)* To tell you the truth, I ain't had a girl-friend since . . .

(Joaquin ponders the time.)

Joaquin: *(continuing)* . . . since second grade when I was in love with Marta Ramirez.

Freddie: What do you mean you were in love with Marta Ramirez?

Joaquin: You know Marta?

Freddie: Yeah, I know her. She was my girl.

Joaquin: Marta with ponytails and pudgy *rodillas*?

Freddie: Marta was in love with me, *ese*.

Joaquin: *Imposible*!

Freddie: What do you mean impossible? She used to give me a burrito sometimes. That's how much she liked me.

Joaquin: That burrito was mine!

Freddie: Your burrito? The one with all the weenies *y huevos*? Plus a splotch of ketchup?

Joaquin: *Claro!* My mom used to make it for me and packed me a whole herd of animal crackers. *(pause)* Me and Marta would suck on their little *patas*, and talk about finger painting and 3 plus 3, *y todo.*

Freddie: *(stunned)* I can't believe Marta was two-timing me in second grade.

(Depressed, Joaquin and Freddie sit down.)

Joaquin: What a *movida* that girl threw on me. My mom used to fix *mi lonche.* Slaved at the stove. Then instead of eating them, I'd go hungry and give them to her.

Freddie: Marta? You sure it was her?

(Joaquin nods his head. Martin breaks the depressing mood and points to the mailbox.)

Martin: Check out the *placas* on the mailbox. Maybe we can get some advice from our ancestors.

Tito: This mailbox is almost as old as the Bible.

(They huddle around the mailbox.)

Joaquin: *(to Freddie)* Dude, ain't this your dad's name?

Freddie: Yeah, it's *mi papi's placa*, but it ain't my mom's name.

Tito: Your dad was a player, *qué no?*

Joaquin: *Quizás. (pause)* Here's all sorts of names. Belinda *con* Ralphie. Sara *con* Julio. Carmen *con* David.

Freddie: Check this out. *Chorizo con huevos!*

(Freddie and Tito slap palms and yuk it up.)

Joaquin: *Mira!* Here's my mom's name. José *con* Patricia.

Tito: I think that "José" is my dad! I recognize his *placa.*

Joaquin: Your dad? Your dad used to like my mom? That's weird, homes. We're almost like brothers. *Hermanos!*

Tito: That's weird alright. And just think. If they had gotten married, we would have never been born. Never existed! This whole Chicano reality would have been nada, *nada!*

Joaquin: I'm glad that my mom dumped your dad.

Martin: *(pointing to another "placa")* This is sound advice. "Don't get fooled by plastic love." *Muy profundo.* Kind of like a Chicano Socrates!

Freddie: *(in a crybaby voice)* That's for sure. Like Marta Ramirez when she gave Joaquin's burrito to me. I feel bad, really low.

Martin: Hold yourself together. Be strong!

Freddie: I'll try. I'm giving us *chucos* a bad name, crying onstage. But it hurts.

Martin: I know it hurts. I've been there.

(Freddie stops crying.)

Martin: That's better.

Tito: *(examining mailbox)* There's all kinds of names. Armando *con* Patricia.

Martin: Patricia *con* Ralphie.

Tito: Ralphie *con* Carolina.

Martin: Carolina *con* Chato. And look at this! Joaquin *con* Susana. Joaquin *con* Susana? *(the three*

60

look at Joaquin) Hey, Romeo, are you this Joaquin?

(Joaquin smiles shyly.)

Tito: Look at him smile his *gran gatito* smile. Is this the Susana that's friends with Ceci?

Joaquin: So?

Martin: That's cool. I like Ceci, and you like Susana, and these *vatos* here are left out in the cold.

(Freddie walks toward the audience, chest stuck out.)

Freddie: *Ni modo.* We can can find a girl anytime.

Tito: *(surprised)* We can?

Freddie: *Simón.* We just . . . call one of those 900 numbers. Or . . . *(scanning the audience)* Hey, that little pumpkin *allá*, she's cute.

Tito: And her over there.

Freddie: And this *muchacha* with the wild hair. What's your number, girl?

Martin: That's enough drooling, you dogs. *(pause)* Let's get on with life. Let me buy you guys a soda. You really fixed me up.

Joaquin: You're allright, bro. Let's go.

61

Martin: Sodas for everyone. Big Gulps with lots of ice!

(They shake hands and all four depart, strutting off the stage. Lights dim as music plays, then darken. Lights come up on Susana and Lupe.)

Lupe: You think there's something wrong with Ceci?

Susana: I don't know. She's sure different, huh? Different from before.

Lupe: When I went to her house, she had a bird feeder, an aquarium, a pet turtle, a butterfly net, and that microscope from the store. She was on her bed and instead of *Lowrider* magazine, she was reading *National Geographic*.

Susana: Ceci has really changed.

Lupe: But you know, maybe she's right about school. We got to study a little more. Maybe we can be nurses.

Susana: Not nurses, doctors!

Lupe: I like that—doctors. We can help our *gente* when they're sick.

Susana: Or maybe we can become veterinarians. Take care of the dogs and cats *en el barrio*.

Lupe: *Claro que sí!* They need help too.

Susana: *(reflecting)* Ceci is just going through a phase in her life. We've got to stick by her.

Lupe: Like peanut butter on a flour *tortilla*. We got to stick!

(Enter Ceci, dressed in a nerdish skirt, with glasses and a calculator. She pushes a cart, which holds a microscope, a chess set, and other scientific props.)

Ceci: *(in mispronounced Spanish)* Hola! Cómo están mis amigas?

(Susana and Lupe look at one another, confused.)

Ceci: How do I look?

Lupe: *(muttering to Susana)* Remember to stick by her. *(to Ceci)* You look really, really . . . different. But good different.

Ceci: I cut my fingernails, too.

Lupe: You didn't! *(examining them)* You did! You had the most beautiful fingernails in *el barrio*.

Susana: Your mascara. It's gone!

Ceci: *Y mi mariposa.*

(She shows her once-tattooed ankle.)

Lupe: You had your tattoo lasered?

Ceci: *(nodding her head)* It's gone. I'm going to snag my nerd. *(from the shopping cart, she brings out item after item)* I got my microscope, my Bunsen burner, my Erlenmeyer flasks, and my chess-board. And I even have a graphing calculator exactly like Martin's!

Lupe: I thought it was kind of big for a pager.

Susana: *(rolling her eyes at Lupe)* I'm sure he'll be impressed.

Ceci: *(taking up two chess pieces)* I'm excited. *(pause)* Did you know that you're not supposed to move your queen until you've made at least three moves? I read it in a book.

(Susana and Lupe yawn at this information.)

Ceci: *(continuing)* And did you know that the queen termite is a thousand times larger than her subjects? *(pause)* Do you think Martin will like me?

Susana: "Like" is not the word. You're a dream come true.

Lupe: Ceci, we're really worried about you. We love you. Why can't you be a homegirl like us no more?

(Ceci looks into the microscope.)

Ceci: If we didn't have the ozone layer in place, cosmic gases could reach earth.

Susana: Sounds *fuchi*.

Lupe: *(to Susana)* We're going to have to do something to bring her back. *(pause)* It's all Sleepy's fault. He treated her like dirt.

Susana: That's for sure.

Lupe: If Ceci goes crazy on us, we'll bring in a *curandera* to help her out.

Susana: Or a priest. Just like when that girl in The Exorcist was twisting her head around and around and acting all weird.

(They twist their heads around.)

Lupe: Stuff like that really happens.

(The boys enter, walking their lowriding strut, aloof to the three girls. They kneel and look tough.)

Martin: *Qué pasa*, homegirls?

Susana: Kicking back. Hanging.

(Martin circles Susana and Lupe.)

Martin: Susana *y* Lupe.

Susana: *(happily)* You know our names?

Martin: Sure. I see you at school.

Lupe: *(flirting)* You go to our school? I don't think I seen you before.

Susana: We would have noticed a pretty face like yours.

(Martin smiles to the audience.)

Martin: Maybe you didn't look hard enough.

Susana: Nah, me and Lupe are always looking. Huh, girl?

Lupe: *Siempre.*

Martin: I was around. You were too busy to

notice. *Soy* Martin Pablo Alvarez Gonzalez de Vaca. But I go by the name of—

(Joaquin steps between them.)

Joaquin: *(to Martin, in a near whisper)* Don't let on who you are. Be calm, *ese.*

(Martin considers the advice.)

Martin: I've been around. I'm what you call a dude with a split personality.

Lupe: That's good. One personality for me and one for Susana.

(Susana and Lupe take hold of Martin's arms, then slowly begin to tug at him. Martin breaks away when Ceci enters. He's struck by Ceci's nerdish beauty. In turn, Ceci is struck by Martin's cholo appearance.)

Ceci: *(nerdishly)* Hi.

(Martin becomes shy.)

Ceci: I said, "Hi." You look remarkably swell!

Martin: *(timidly)* Who, me?

(Martin hides behind Joaquin.)

Joaquin: What's wrong? This ain't the first day of kindergarten. Don't be shy.

Martin: *(to Joaquin)* She's so pretty.

(Joaquin looks her up and down.)

Joaquin: Whatever moves you. If you think she's cute, then get in there. Show her your Chicano magnetism.

Martin: I can't! Look at me. I'm a *cholo* and she's so *(to the audience)* . . . so perfect.

(Lights darken.)

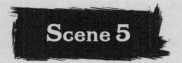

Scene 5

A high school classroom with desks, a globe, a flag, etc. The teacher, a mannequin-like figure, sits behind the desk.

(Lights come up, stage right. Martin, newly made cholo, *skims through a school yearbook.)*

Martin: I can't find her in the yearbook. It's not Gloria. Or Iris. Maybe it's this girl with her eyes closed. I hate it when you take a picture with your eyes like this *(closing eyes)* or sometimes your face is like this . . .

(Martin makes an ugly face at the audience, then returns his attention to the yearbook.)

Martin: *(continuing)* It's not her either. *(slamming the yearbook closed)* I've been in high school for three years. I can't believe I didn't notice her before. She's a real beautiful nerd girl and I'm, *pues*, check me out. A *cholo*. A *cholo* for life.

(Martin pulls at his Pendleton, but it refuses to come off. He's wearing a hairnet and he tugs at it, but it too refuses to come off.)

Martin: *Y mis garras!* They won't come off. I'm stuck in this reality.

(Joaquin, now dressed as a nerd, tiptoes into the classroom, but stops in his tracks. Late for class, he addresses his teacher.)

Joaquin: I'm sorry I'm late, Mrs. Ponce. Stay after school? But I got a good lie, I mean, a good reason. My stupid little brother ate a whole box of crayons. I had to drive him over to emergency. I promise, it won't happen again. *(pause as he listens to his teacher)* Thanks, Mrs. Ponce. I won't let the punk eat crayons again.

(Relieved that he's off the hook, Joaquin takes a seat.)

Martin: *Qué pasó?* What's going on with you?

Joaquin: Nothing.

Martin: What do you mean nothing? How come you're dressed like that?

Joaquin: *(shyly)* I want to be a nerd too.

Martin: Get out of here.

Joaquin: *En serio*. I got me an ant farm just like you.

Martin: I'm going to hit you, man.

Joaquin: You know that nerd girl we saw yesterday?

(Martin nods his head.)

Joaquin: I like her a lot.

Martin: What! You can't like her!

(Joaquin gets Martin into a headlock, but lets go to direct his attention to the teacher.)

Joaquin: No, Mrs. Ponce, we ain't fighting. I was searching his head for lice. For *piojos*. They run in his family.

Martin: Yeah, on my dad's side.

(Martin and Joaquin smile at the teacher.)

Martin: You can't like her. I like her!

Joaquin: You got Ceci.

(Martin considers Joaquin's remark.)

Martin: When did this happen?

Joaquin: Last night, in bed. *(hesitant)* Man, I never really had a girlfriend.

Martin: What are you saying?

Joaquin: I said, I never really had a girlfriend. I'm telling you the truth. I put on like I'm all *suave*, all bad, but I ain't! And all the fights I got into, heck, I lost them all.

Martin: *(concerned)* What are you saying?

Joaquin: I'm saying that I think I got a chance with this nerd girl. I thought maybe her ants would like to kick around with my ants. *Tú sabes?*

Martin: *Imposible.* I got my eye on her.

Joaquin: But you're a *cholo*. Anyhow, you wanted Ceci. You got to make up your mind.

(Martin appears downcast.)

Martin: All my life I've been waiting for a girl like her to show up, and finally when she does, *pues*, I'm not her type no more. I'm this other person, and I can't change.

Joaquin: *(referring to the yearbook)* What you got there, homes? I mean, *(nerdishly)* what is that you're perusing so intently?

Martin: The yearbook. She's got to be here.

(Joaquin stares at Martin's hairnet.)

Joaquin: Your hairnet's cool. I been a nerd *(looking at watch)* for only three hours, and I miss being a *cholo*. *Pero* those days are gone.

(Freddie and Tito enter, tiptoeing.)

Freddie: I'm sorry I'm late, Mrs. Ponce. My *mocoso* brother ate some crayons. I had to take his little *nalgas* down to emergency.

Tito: *(to teacher)* And I had to go with the dude for moral and spiritual support. Nah, we won't be late ever again 'cause Freddie's brother ate the whole box. What, Mrs. Ponce? That was Joaquin's excuse? *(to Joaquin)* Hey, man, you're always stealing our excuses. Get your own— *(becoming aware of Joaquin's clothes)* Why you dressed like that?

(Freddie and Tito are struck by Joaquin's nerdish

attire. They mouth their amazement as lights fade. Lights come up, stage left, on the same classroom configuration of chairs, globe, flag, etc. But hanging behind them is a portrait of Martin as nerd and the caption "Student of the Year." Ceci, Lupe, and Susana are seated, secretly munching on french fries.)

Ceci: *(dreamily)* That new guy! He was one delicious-looking brown item on the menu.

Lupe: Like the best dish on the menu.

Ceci: A hot *tamal.*

Susana: Just like these french fries.

Lupe: *Cómo?*

Susana: Didn't you notice his cool walk? Sort of like this.

(Susana takes two french fries and scissors them like walking legs.)

Ceci: That's cute, Susana. But he's much more impressive than french fries. I was born for him.

Susana: But you have your eye on Martin.

Ceci: *(downcast)* I know I said I liked him. But I liked this other guy too.

74

Lupe: You can't have them all. Leave some for us. You take Junior Einstein, and me and Susana, we'll fight over this dude.

Susana: The best *chola* wins.

(They shake hands. Ceci stands up and paces.)

Ceci: You're right. Now look at me. I'm caught in this role that I invented for myself. *(to the teacher as she sits back down)* Sorry, Mrs. Sierra. *(pulling at back of skirt)* I had to stand up because I had a wedgie.

Lupe: I knew this would come back on you. Just when you gave up on *vatos locos*, here's one worth keeping.

Ceci: There's something about him. He looks familiar, *qué no?* Like we seen him before?

Lupe: I had that feeling *también*.

(Lupe turns and studies the portrait of Martin as Student of the Year. She gets up from her desk and approaches it.)

Lupe: The new *vato* kind of looks like Martin. Nah, it can't be. *(to the teacher)* Why am I out of my seat? Uh, I'm sraightening the picture. You know how us Rams [or local school mascot] have our school pride.

(Lupe sits back down and leans over Ceci's shoulder, as they flip through the yearbook.)

Ceci: Check the yearbook again. He's got to be in here.

(The bell rings for recess. Lights come up, stage right, where the boys are now standing by their desks. Susana and Lupe walk to the middle of the stage while Ceci hovers in the back among her scientific equipment. Susana and Lupe approach Joaquin, struck by his nerdish attire.)

Susana: *(to Joaquin)* What's with you, homeboy? Did you go to a slumber party at Junior Einstein's house?

(Joaquin turns away, and Martin steps forward.)

Lupe: *(to Susana)* There he is!

(Susana and Lupe take hold of Martin and begin to pull on him. He breaks away.)

76

Martin: *Cálmate!*

(Martin turns to dust the portrait of himself as Student of the Year.)

Martin: I heard of this dude. Good things *también*.

Lupe: He ain't nowhere. *(pause)* We looked in the yearbook, but we couldn't find you.

Martin: I'm there. Did you check out the science club?

(Susana and Lupe shake their heads.)

Martin: I was invisible to you two, all because I was different. Let me give you a hint.

(He pulls back his Pendleton to display his calculator. The girls are shocked.)

Lupe: Impressive calculator.

Martin: *(closing his Pendleton)* Be cool, girl. There is a time and place for playing with my calculator.

Susana: You can't be. You're not—Martin? The Chicano nerd?

Martin: The former Chicano nerd. I had a heart transplant, but I kept my math skills intact. *(gesturing to Joaquin.) Mis carnales* fixed me all up.

Joaquin: It's true. Took a little Bondo to his *cuerpo, y* presto, you had one of these—

Tito: *(butting in)* Transmissions, huh?

Joaquin: Transformations, *tonto*! How many times do I got to tell you?

(Lupe and Susana flirt outrageously with Martin.)

Lupe: You're looking really good, Martin.

Susana: I saw him first.

Lupe: *Mentirosa*, I did!

(Martin waves off Susana and Lupe.)

Martin: I'm going to be direct. I'm looking for Ceci Cortez, the Little Red Riding Hood *de mi corazón. (downcast)* Also, I got my eye on that pretty nerd girl. She was with you yesterday.

(Ceci steps forward, ready to leap into his arms.)

Lupe: *(eyeing Ceci)* She's busy right now.

Susana: Real busy.

(Martin eyes nerdish Ceci.)

Martin: *(to the audience)* The dilemma. Two types of loves. But here's my one chance. Ceci would be fine, *pero* I'm attracted to this item *también*.

(Martin approaches her slowly, but Joaquin pushes his way between them.)

Joaquin: *(nerdishly, to Ceci)* Hi, cutie!

(Ceci pushes him out of her way.)

Joaquin: *(stomping his foot)* I'm never going to snag a girl.

(Freddie and Tito comfort Joaquin.)

Martin: *(to Ceci)* Girl, you look *muy* familiar.

Ceci: No, I'm just your basic nerd.

Martin: No, there's something special.

(Martin pulls her sweater aside, revealing a calculator.)

Martin: *(continuing)* Cool calculator.

Ceci: It's a Texas Instrument, model TI95.

(Martin eyes the shopping cart loaded with scientific equipment.)

Martin: And your chess set, and your microscope. *(pause)* You haven't seen this *chola* named Ceci? She called one of my homeboys *(pointing to Tito)* a bad word when they were in second grade.

Tito: *(in a crybaby voice)* She made me cry when she called me a *"caca."* That mean ol' Ceci.

Ceci: No, I haven't met her yet. But I hear she's a really nice girl.

Martin: Yeah, well, I like her, and I, you know, *(muttering)* I like you *también*.

Joaquin: This is sorry. I been a *cholo* all my life and after one day he's getting them all.

Ceci: *(to Martin)* You do? You like me?

Martin: And I like your glasses.

Ceci: You know how to flatter a girl.

Lupe: *(steaming)* Hey, I saw the *vato* first, Ceci!

(Lupe covers her mouth, having let the cat out of the bag. Everyone appears shocked. Martin circles Ceci.)

Martin: Ceci? *(pause)* I used to have a crush on you when I was a Chicano nerd. I used to look in my microscope and I couldn't concentrate on all the bacteria and germs. You were taking over my life, *mi vida*. Then tears would fall from my eyes, ninety-six *lágrimas*.

Ceci: I felt the same, Martin. Sometimes when I was listening to the radio, I pictured you in the songs.

Martin: You liked me back then?

Ceci: I did. And I do now.

(Ceci sings a portion of the nerdish song.)

Ceci: Molecules, fluctuating molecules,/floating in the calculus of our feelings.

Martin: I love that oldie but goodie. *(pause)* We've changed. Look at me, Ceci, and look at yourself. Maybe we could slip out of these *trajes*. We can meet halfway.

Ceci: Here on the stage? People are looking.

Martin: *(to the audience)* Close your eyes. No peeking.

(Ceci removes her eyeglasses and steps out of her billowy dress into a sleek aerobic outfit. Martin takes off his Pendleton and fits a tie around his neck. He puts on fashionable eyewear.)

Martin: *(to the audience)* OK, open *sus ojos*! *(to Ceci)* You heard of Romeo and Juliet. They ain't nothing compared to us. We're the real thing.

Susana: That's so romantic.

(Susana leans against Joaquin's shoulder. Freddie and Tito place their heads against each other. They push away after they realize what they're doing.)

Ceci: *(to Joaquin)* Susana saw your name and hers together on the mailbox. It said, "Joaquin *con* Susana."

(Susana jumps away from Joaquin's shoulder.)

Martin: *Adelante!* Go, *tigre*. Tell Susana your feelings.

Joaquin: But I'm dressed *(looking at himself)* like this.

Martin: Go for it, dude. Don't let your *garras* keep you back.

(Joaquin walks up to Susana in a low-slow walk.)

Joaquin: *(in a mousey voice)* Hi, cutie pie. *(clearing, then deepening his voice)* Qué pasa, paloma? You looking *muy fina*.

Susana: Why are you dressed like that?

Joaquin: I can't really explain. But I can explain how I feel.

Susana: *Ay, qué macho!* I saw your name on the mailbox. You spelled "eternally" wrong. You sure your feelings are true?

Joaquin: Baby, I'm for real—r-e-e-l.

Susana: That's close enough.

(They sway arm in arm as in a dance)

Tito: What about us? Me and Freddie! We never get nobody!

Lupe: *(beckoning with a finger)* Hey, Freddie. I used to have a crush on your older brother. He's in the Marines, *qué no*?

Freddie: He's a barber in the Marines now. But when I go, I'm going to drive a tank. I'm going to throw my switch and hop my tank.

(He hops his body as he pretends to hit the hydraulics of a lowrider.)

Lupe: *(leaning on his shoulder)* Qué ambition!

(Freddie hurries to the chalkboard and sounds out the words as he writes "Freddie con Lupe.")

Tito: This is sorry. I feel bad. There ain't nobody for me. It's the story *de mi vida*. I never get to write "Tito *con* Gloria" or "Tito *con* Maya" or "Tito *con* Araceli". I didn't even get to say the "*chorizo con huevos*" line.

(The couples begin to dance slowly. Tito pouts.)

Tito: *(continuing)* Everyone's got somebody except me. My mom has my dad, and my dad has his beer and TV. My sister has somebody, and you guys got something sweet happening. Even my dog Humo has a girl dog, a little poodle from down the block. *(scaning the audience)* Espérate! Wait a minute. Hey, there's one out there for me. *Chihuahua,* I see her. You got a boyfriend? *Ven acá!* Come here, girl . . .

(Tito brings a girl up from the audience. He asks her name and he takes her hand. The couples part. They sing part of the nerdish song.)

Together: Molecules, fluctuating molecules,/ floating in the calculus of our feelings.

(Lights dim, then darken.)

END

Selected Spanish, Caló, and brand-name words used in *Nerdlandia*;

Informal definitions:

allá   over there
asco   nauseous feeling
bolas   dollars
Bondo   plasterlike material for filling in car dents
cállate!   be quiet!
cálmate!   calm down!
carnal(es)   brother(s), blood brother(s)
chale   no way
chingasos   punches, as in fighting
chisme   gossip
chones   underwear
chucos   from pachucos; zoot suiters
claro que sí   of course
cochino   dirty
con safos   a sign-off on graffiti; a sort of "amen"
cuento   story
cuerpo   body
cuidado!   careful!
curandera   healer
de veras   truthfully
en serio   seriously
espérate!   wait a minute!

feo   ugly
fíjate!   look here!
flaca   skinny
fuchi   smelly
garras   clothes; rags
gorro   hat
güero   person of light complexion
híjole   oh, wow
huevones   lazy persons
jefe   boss; father
jeta   long face
lágrimas   tears
mariposa   butterfly
mentirosos   liars
mira este chavalo!   look at this boy!
mocoso   snotty person
movida   secret plan
muy lejos   very far
nalgas   butt; fanny
nel   no
ni modo   no way
novio   boyfriend
órale   all right
paleta   popsicle
panadería   bakery
patas   legs
placa   graffiti mark; signature

pleitos   fights
puro pedo   pure nonsense
qué piensas?   what do you think?
qué quibo?   how goes it?
rasgüachi   something in shambles
rodillas   knees
simón   that's right
sinvergüenza   without shame
sustos   bad spirits
tapado   stuck up
tonto   dummy
trajes   clothes
triste   sad
tú sabes   you know
vatos locos   crazy dudes
ven   come on
yo creo   I believe